A BLACK BELT'S GUIDE TO RULES IN LIFE

(THEY DIDN'T TELL YOU ABOUT)

WRITTEN BY

JASON FIGLIANO

LiveLife**Happy**
Publishing

Published and Distributed in Canada by Live Life Happy Publishing.
www.livelifehappypublishing.com

Library of Congress Cataloging-in-Publication Data

Jason Figliano

A Black Belt's Guide to Rules in Life (They Didn't Tell You About)

Self-Help / Personal Growth / Happiness / Body, Mind & Spirit / Inspiration & Personal Growth / Self-Help / Spiritual / Mindfulness & Meditation

ISBN: 978-1-998724-22-2 Paperback

ISBN: 978-1-998724-23-9 Electronic Book

Cover Design: Jason Figliano

Live Life Happy Publishing

PUBLISHER'S NOTE & AUTHOR DISCLAIMER

This publication is designed to provide accurate and authoritative information concerning the subject matter covered. It is sold to understand that the publisher and author are not engaging in or rendering any psychological, medical or other professional services. If expert assistance or counselling is needed, seek the services of a competent medical professional. For immediate support call your local crisis line. The following book could contain actual events and experiences that the author has encountered in their life. However, some names and specific locations have been changed or omitted to protect the privacy and confidentiality of the individuals involved. The changes do not alter the story's integrity or its messages.

DEDICATION

To every student I've ever taught—and every teacher I've ever learned from.
Your lessons, your failures, your courage, and your resilience live within these pages.
This is for the warriors who show up, fall down, and rise stronger—not just in the dojo, but in life.

To my past self—the young man who didn't have the answers, but kept showing up anyway.
And to the reader holding this book:
May these rules find you when you need them most, and may you carry them with strength, clarity, and heart.

For the one in 10,000.
The one who trains when no one is watching.
Who takes the hits, swallows the ego, sharpens the mind, and stands up anyway.
This is your guide—not because life gets easier, but because you get stronger.

TABLE OF CONTENT

PREFACE

When I first connected with Jason Figliano, I knew instantly that he wasn't just a martial artist—he was a **lifelong learner, a leader, and a living example of resilience, wisdom, and integrity.**

As the founder of Live Life Happy Publishing, I have the joy and honor of working with passionate authors who want to make a real impact in the world. And let me tell you—**Jason is one of those authors.**

With over three decades of experience in martial arts, Jason has trained, taught, led, and lived a life rooted in discipline, humility, and heart. He's not only a **6th-degree black belt in Shotokan Kempo Karate** and a **3rd-degree black belt in Gracie Jiu-Jitsu** under *Master Royler Gracie*, but also an **entrepreneur, educator, and community builder.** His Canadian Black Belt Academy has been voted the best martial arts school in Caledon for twelve years in a row—not because of flashy techniques, but because of the **character and leadership** he brings into every class, every interaction, every moment.

This book isn't a martial arts manual. It's a **life manual**. It's for anyone navigating the challenges of everyday living—from parenting and heartbreak to business and burnout. Jason pulls back the curtain on the unspoken rules that most people are never taught—but desperately need. Through the metaphor of belt ranks and the real-life arenas we all face, he hands us the wisdom we often wish we had learned sooner.

And that's exactly why I believe this book is so important. **Jason has lived these lessons. He's earned every word**—not just through his achievements, but through his setbacks, his self-reflection, and his deep desire to help others rise.

If you're holding this book, you're in for a powerful journey. You'll be challenged. You'll be inspired. And if you stick with it—just like a white belt who never quits—you'll walk away stronger, more centered, and ready to take on life with black belt-level clarity.

Welcome to the dojo. Welcome to the pages that might just change the way you show up in the world.

Let's get to work.

Andrea Seydel
Founder & CEO
Live Life Happy Publishing

INTRODUCTION

Why I Wrote This Book

Throughout my journey in martial arts, I've encountered countless individuals seeking more than just physical training—they're searching for life principles that resonate beyond the dojo. This book is a culmination of the lessons I've learned, taught, and lived. It's designed to guide you, the reader, through the challenges of life using the foundational principles of martial arts: humility, discipline, courage, and legacy.

I aim to provide a roadmap for personal growth, drawing parallels between the belt progression in martial arts and the stages of life's journey. Whether you're a seasoned martial artist or someone seeking direction, I hope this book serves as a beacon, illuminating the path to personal mastery and fulfillment.

Why We Begin on the Mat

"A black belt is just a white belt who never quit." – Unknown

Not all martial arts systems use the same colors. Some skip ranks. Some reorder them. Some add stripes or different paths. But every one of them starts the same way—with a **white belt**—and for the rare few who stay the course, they end in **black**... and maybe, someday, **red**.

This book follows that path.

But make no mistake—this isn't a book about martial arts. It's about **life**. It begins in the dojo because that's where **discipline**, **humility**, and **truth** first take root.

A dojo, by definition, is a place of practice—a training hall, a sanctuary for becoming. It's where we learn to fall. To get back up. To spar without ego. To master ourselves under pressure. You don't need to have worn a gi or stepped onto the mat to understand these lessons. Because the real fight was never against another person. It was always against your own excuses.

Inside these pages are **nine chapters**, each one set in a different arena of life:

- The dojo
- The street
- The competition mat
- Warfare
- The roadside
- The breakup
- The parenting journey
- The moment you're losing
- And the moment you've lost everything

Each chapter holds **nine rules**. But more than that, each **Rule #1** across all chapters speaks to the same core principle: **Humility**. Rule #2? **Discipline**. Rule #3? **Courage**. And so on—through **Ego**, **Control**, **Responsibility**, **Mastery**, **Legacy in Action**, and **Legacy in Spirit**.

Those nine rules? They reflect the **nine belt ranks** that form the heart of this book's structure:

1. **White** – Humility
2. **Yellow** – Discipline
3. **Orange** – Courage
4. **Green** – Ego
5. **Purple** – Control
6. **Blue** – Responsibility
7. **Brown** – Mastery
8. **Black** – Legacy in Action
9. **Red and Black** – Legacy in Spirit
10. **Red** – Constant and Never-ending Improvement

Most readers will resonate with some rules more than others. That's natural. You may already be living Rule #4 but neglecting Rule #1. You may have mastered how to lose but not how to raise a child. You may be wearing a "black belt" in one part of life—and still fumbling with your white belt in another.

That's okay. That's real.

Because these rules weren't pulled from a manual, they were **earned** through failure, loss, crisis, recovery, late nights, early mornings, and the long walk back after getting knocked down.

This book is meant to feel like the training floor. Not because you'll sweat, but because it asks something of you:

- **To reflect.**
- **To be honest.**
- **To challenge what you've accepted.**
- **To become harder to kill—and easier to respect.**

And like martial arts itself, this path isn't for everyone.

Let me show you why.

For every 10,000 people who begin martial arts:

- 5,000 quit in the first six months
- 1,000 last a year
- 500 train for two
- 100 reach three years
- 10 earn a first-degree black belt
- And **1 or 2** ever reach second-degree

Red belt? That's one in 10,000.

But belts aren't just earned on mats. They're earned in boardrooms, bedrooms, battlefields, and breakdowns. They're earned every time you **choose the hard right over the easy wrong.**

So the question this book asks isn't whether these rules are "good."

The question is:

Will you be the one who lives them?

Let's begin where all black belts start:
The mat.
The sweat.
The first lesson.

Welcome to the dojo. Let's get to work.

A martial arts way to reading reading this book:

Read This Book Like a Black Belt

This isn't a book meant to be rushed through in one sitting. Each chapter is like a belt rank—earned, not just read. Take the time to sit with each section. Read it slowly. Reflect on what hits you. Apply it. Let it challenge your habits, your beliefs, your actions.

Much like martial arts training, you're not just advancing—you're constantly reviewing. As you progress to the next belt, you continue practicing and refining the lessons from the previous one. This book should be treated the same way.

Before you move on to the next chapter, return to the last. Revisit it. Test it. See where it shows up in your life.

Mastery doesn't come from moving fast. It comes from moving with purpose.

This is A Black Belt's Guide—not The guide—because it comes from my personal experience as a lifelong martial artist, school owner, and black belt.

The rules in this book are based on what I've learned through training, teaching, winning, losing, and leading. You may have different views—and that's okay.

This isn't about being right. It's about being real.

Take what resonates. Leave what doesn't. And keep showing up.

WHITE BELT

CHAPTER 1
RULES IN THE DOJO
(THEY DIDN'T TELL YOU ABOUT)

*"The more you sweat in training, the less
you bleed in battle." – Unknown*

*"The dojo is not a place to impress.
It is a place to improve." – Anonymous*

Introduction

Before we talk about life, war, heartbreak, parenting, or loss—
we start in the dojo.

Why?

Because the **dojo** is more than a room with mats and walls.
In Japanese, "dojo" literally means "place of the way." It's the
sacred space where discipline is forged, humility is tested, and
the ego gets stripped bare. It's where belts are earned, not given.
Where you confront your limits, and sometimes, your excuses.

Some dojos smell like sweat and hard mats. Others are spotless and silent. Some are in strip malls. Some are in basements. But the truth is, your dojo isn't just a building—it's wherever you go to sharpen yourself.

And if you've never stepped into one? That's okay. Because the rules that govern the dojo are the same rules that govern life—if you're paying attention. They weren't written on the walls. They were embedded in black eyes, sore ribs, and quiet nods from teachers who didn't hand out easy praise.

This is where we begin. In the dojo. At white belt. Where every lesson starts.

1. Bow when you enter. *(Humility)*

Every session starts the same: you bow. Not for tradition's sake—but to remind yourself this space is different. The bow isn't for the instructor. It's for you. A silent declaration: *"I'm here to learn."*

In the dojo, no one cares about your titles, your bank account, or your social media. The mat is the great equalizer. A lawyer and a janitor can both get choked by a 16-year-old white belt. It's not status that wins here—it's humility. The willingness to admit you don't know. The courage to listen instead of talk. The grace to start over when your technique falls apart.

Humility isn't weakness. It's strength without noise. It's what separates those who grow from those who just perform.

But here's what it looks like when you ignore this: You walk in with ego. You compare belts. You size up your partners. And soon, you're rolling with a chip on your shoulder instead of an open mind. You tap too late. You blame the mat. You quit when corrected. And the mat teaches you the hard way: pride takes longer to tap than pain.

2. Line up before class. *(Discipline)*

Before every class, students line up in belt order. No excuses. No chaos. Just structure.

That line is about more than tradition—it's about discipline. Showing up on time. Wearing the proper uniform, knowing your place, not in a hierarchy of people, but in a system of earned progress.

Discipline in the dojo isn't a flash of motivation—it's the quiet repetition of good habits. Tying your belt the same way. Warming up with purpose and drilling the basics without boredom.

That consistency spills into life. When you line up without being told, you start waking up without hitting the snooze button. You meal prep. You plan. You train. Discipline isn't restrictive—it's freedom earned through structure.

But here's what it looks like when you ignore this: You show up late. You forget your belt. You skip warmups. You wait to "feel ready" before putting in effort. And soon, that pattern bleeds into your work, your health, and your relationships. Without discipline, chaos creeps in—and so does regret.

3. Accept that you'll be tapped out. *(Courage)*

You will lose. A lot.

No matter how strong or skilled you are, someone will choke you, sweep you, submit you. And the more you avoid it, the more you stunt your growth.

Courage in the dojo isn't about being fearless—it's about stepping in knowing you might get humbled. Again. And again. It's about staying on the mat when your chest is tight, when your confidence is shaky, when your instincts scream, "fake an injury and go home."

That courage is the same one you'll need in every tough conversation, every big decision, every new start in life. The mat trains your courage by testing your limits in a controlled storm.

But here's what it looks like when you ignore this: You duck hard rolls. You cherry-pick partners. You quit mid-spar. And you tell yourself it's smart, not scared. But your fear grows in the shadow of avoidance. Until one day, life taps you—and you're unprepared to respond.

4. Respect isn't asked for—it's modeled. *(Ego)*

The black belt doesn't demand bows—they earn them.

In the dojo, ego makes you loud. But respect makes you consistent. The most dangerous person in the room is usually the quietest. They don't puff their chest. They don't correct others to be seen. They lead by example—by how they move, how they speak, how they fail with dignity.

Your ego will want credit. Recognition. Validation. But the dojo reminds you: real respect comes when you serve the class, not yourself.

But here's what it looks like when you ignore this: You brag about your taps. You correct others to feel smart. You challenge higher belts for clout. And when people stop respecting you, you confuse fear for admiration. You might win rounds—but you lose the room.

5. Breathe when you panic. *(Control)*

Sparring isn't just physical—it's psychological. And panic is always waiting.

You gas out in a bad position. You forget the escape. Your heart rate spikes. Your vision narrows. And in that moment, you have a choice: flail or breathe.

Control begins with breath. You inhale through discomfort. Exhale into the moment. It's what allows you to think while under pressure, to transition when you want to freeze. Breath leads to clarity. And clarity leads to survival.

But here's what it looks like when you ignore this: You thrash. You hold your breath. You waste energy in bad positions. And you get caught—not because you were outclassed, but because you surrendered to panic. In the dojo and in life, breath is the first thing stress steals. Take it back.

6. Clean the mats. *(Responsibility)*

After class, you clean. Not because you made the mess. But because this is your space.

Wiping the mats isn't about germs—it's about ownership. You contribute. You care. You give back without being told.

Responsibility means you don't just show up for yourself. You show up for the culture. For the next class. For the student walking in for the first time. It's leadership at its most basic: serve before you're served.

But here's what it looks like when you ignore this: You leave early. You step over trash. You treat the dojo like a service instead of a community. And slowly, the culture erodes. The class becomes about consumption, not contribution. You stop being a student and become a parasite.

7. Drill the basics. *(Mastery)*

The black belt didn't invent a secret move—they just mastered the fundamentals.

Shrimping. Bridging. Hip escapes. You'll do them a thousand times. And then a thousand more. Because mastery isn't boredom—it's depth. You find nuance where others see repetition. You find excellence where others see monotony.

Mastery is doing the boring stuff beautifully.

But here's what it looks like when you ignore this: You skip warmups. You roll instead of drilling. You chase advanced techniques without mastering position. And in doing so, you become flashy—but fragile. You look skilled—until someone pressures you. Then it all falls apart.

8. You are always someone's first impression.
(Legacy in Action)

Every time you roll, someone's watching. Maybe it's a kid. A new student. A visitor is thinking about joining.

They see how you treat lower belts, how you tap, how you teach. And long after they forget your technique, they'll remember your demeanor.

Legacy isn't a speech. It's a pattern. And in the dojo, your actions ripple longer than your accolades.

But here's what it looks like when you ignore this: You big-dog white belts. You hoard techniques. You roll with ego. And students leave—not because of your skill, but because of your attitude. You don't build the next generation—you scare them away.

9. The mat remembers everything. *(Legacy in Spirit)*

You can fake a lot in life, but not here.

The mat remembers who you helped, who you avoided. Who you tapped gently and who you cranked. It remembers who quit when they lost and who laughed through pressure. It's not magical—it's just honest. Like soil, it reflects what you plant.

Years from now, when your belt is frayed and your name is barely mentioned, someone will roll on the same mat and ask about you. What they hear won't be about your technique, but your character.

But here's what it looks like when you ignore this: You think the mat forgets. You think your talent erases your tantrums. But the dojo whispers. And long after your victories are forgotten, your attitude remains part of its culture, for better or worse.

End of Chapter Reflection: The Mat Never Lies

It's 9:45 pm. Class is over. The kids are gone. The music stopped. The room smells like effort and resolve.

You sweep the mats. Your belt is soaked. Your ego is silent. And you replay the night—not the taps, but the lessons.

You bowed in—not just to the space, but to the process (**Rule 1**). You lined up. Showed up. Honored the grind (**Rule 2**).

You lost a round but didn't quit. You stayed present through doubt (**Rule 3**).

You listened more than you spoke. You offered help instead of praise (**Rule 4**). You caught yourself panicking and chose breath over frenzy (**Rule 5**). You stayed after and wiped the mats for someone who left early (**Rule 6**).

You repped the basics again—and found something new in them (**Rule 7**). A new student watched you roll with grace. They'll be back—because of you (**Rule 8**). And the mat under your feet? It says nothing. But it remembers everything. (**Rule 9**)

This is the dojo. And this is where your real life training begins.

YELLOW BELT

CHAPTER 2
RULES IN A STREET FIGHT
(THEY DIDN'T TELL YOU ABOUT)

"Everyone has a plan until they get punched in the mouth." –
Mike Tyson "The best defense is to not be there." – Sun Tzu

Introduction

Street fights are not romantic. They're not choreographed. They're not a movie. They are fast, chaotic, and unforgiving. There are no mats, no referees, and no honor codes. You don't get to tap. You don't get a rematch. You get consequences. Scars. Maybe even charges.

But the rules still exist—even here. They're unspoken, primal, and brutal. And while martial arts prepares you for discipline and form, the street teaches you improvisation and instinct. These aren't rules about technique. They're about survival—mental, physical, and legal.

Here's what a street fight will teach you—if you live through it.

1. Your ego gets you in. Humility gets you out. *(Humility)*

The person who escalates usually regrets it. The moment you start thinking, "I can take this guy," you're already compromised. Humility in a street fight isn't weakness—it's wisdom. It's recognizing that even if you *can* win, it doesn't mean it's worth the cost.

You don't know what they're carrying. Who they're with. What their background is. You might win the fight and lose your freedom. You might lose the fight and wake up in a hospital—or not at all.

Humility means disengaging early. It means walking away, not because you're scared, but because you're smart enough to know the battlefield isn't worth the blood. That kind of restraint takes more strength than swinging first.

But here's what it looks like when you ignore this: You puff up. You mouth off. You think being right means you're untouchable. And in doing so, you write a check your body might not cash. You lose your teeth, your job, or your future—all for proving a point that didn't need proving.

2. You fight how you train. Sloppiness shows under stress. *(Discipline)*

In a real fight, adrenaline hijacks your body. Fine motor skills vanish. You won't rise to the occasion—you'll fall to your level of preparation. That's why discipline matters.

If you've drilled clean technique, it will show. If you've practiced awareness, you'll move early. If you've conditioned your body and sharpened your mindset, you'll keep your feet when others panic.

You don't need to be fancy. You need to be fluent, calm in chaos, and clear in confusion. Street fights punish hesitation and sloppiness. But discipline builds the habits that show up when fear hits.

But here's what it looks like when you ignore this: You throw wild punches. You flinch when things escalate. You get tunnel vision. Your breathing's off. You burn out in seconds and collapse when the moment stretches longer than your comfort zone ever prepared you for.

3. Courage is staying calm when chaos starts. *(Courage)*

Most people freeze. Their fight-or-flight kicks in and chooses *neither.* Courage isn't some raging aggression—it's poise under pressure. It's controlling your heartbeat, managing your breathing, and seeing everything when the world goes blurry.

It's stepping between a friend and danger. It's calling 911 while others yell. It's defusing with presence before it ever becomes a brawl. And when it *does* pop off, it's moving first, moving right, and moving smart.

Courage in a street fight is a survival tool—not a stunt. It doesn't look like a hero monologue. It looks like someone who's done the reps in the dark so they can perform in the chaos.

But here's what it looks like when you ignore this: You freeze. You yell. You swing blind and panic easy. You forget to breathe. And you become part of the problem—not the person who ends it.

4. There is no honor in court. *(Ego)*

You might think you were justified. You might be right. But the law doesn't care about who won the chest-thumping contest. It cares about who swung first. Who kept going. Who had a weapon. Who walked away and who didn't.

Ego makes you escalate. Ego makes you want to "teach a lesson." But the only lesson you'll learn is how quickly your image of being the bigger man ends in legal bills and a criminal record.

Want to really protect yourself? Let your ego die before someone else buries it.

But here's what it looks like when you ignore this: You keep going after they're down. You gloat. You post online. You brag at the bar. And then the video shows up in court. Your lawyer sighs. The judge doesn't care about your side of the story. And suddenly, you're not the badass. You're the defendant.

5. Control starts before contact. *(Control)*

The best fighters win before they throw a punch. They assess, de-escalate, and redirect. Control means spotting trouble early—before it lands in your lap. It means standing tall, speaking clearly, and managing space. It means staying just outside arm's reach, positioning near exits, never letting your back turn.

If it escalates, control means breathing through the panic and using what's necessary—stopping when the threat is neutralized. Not losing yourself in the chaos.

A calm person in a volatile situation holds power. And that power can end fights before they begin—or ensure they end quickly.

But here's what it looks like when you ignore this: You get sucked into the noise. You yell. You get too close. You forget your surroundings. And suddenly you're on the ground, someone's behind you, and you have no idea how you got there.

6. Your actions become evidence. *(Responsibility)*

In the age of cellphones and security cameras, everything you do is recorded by someone, somewhere. That punch you threw? That stomp? That angry scream? All admissible. And worse—interpretable.

Responsibility means acting like everything you do could be played back to your mother, your kids, or a judge. It means using force with clarity, not rage. It means owning your part in the moment—and afterward.

Because real warriors know this: you don't just answer to your opponent. You answer to the consequences.

But here's what it looks like when you ignore this: You act on impulse. You throw first and think later. You leave someone bleeding in the street and run. But the footage comes out. Your face goes viral. And your side of the story is reduced to a headline you can't rewrite.

7. If you fumble in practice, you bleed in real life. *(Mastery)*

A street fight exposes everything you skipped. That one time you didn't train clinch escapes. That drill you always half-assed. That habit of dropping your left hand. It all shows up.

Mastery is a commitment to precision under pressure. It's knowing where to strike and where to stop. It's the footwork that keeps you upright, the hands that stay high, the mind that remains present.

The street doesn't care how tough you *say* you are. It reveals how much you've trained. Or haven't.

But here's what it looks like when you ignore this: You gas out. You slip on gravel. You hit wrong and break your hand. You hesitate at the worst moment. And you realize: your confidence wasn't mastery. It was arrogance in disguise.

8. You teach others how to handle chaos. *(Legacy in Action)*

Your little brother is watching. Your students might be nearby. Maybe even your child. How you conduct yourself in conflict becomes their blueprint.

Legacy isn't built in peaceful moments—it's forged in chaos. You can be the example that says, "You don't need to swing first." Or you can be the cautionary tale they whisper about later.

Someone will learn from your response. Make sure it's worth copying.

But here's what it looks like when you ignore this: You snap. You explode. You swing and scream and leave a trail of mess. And the people who looked up to you? They shrink back, confused. You didn't teach them strength. You taught them how to lose control.

9. Win or lose—the way you carry it becomes your story. *(Legacy in Spirit)*

Whether you walk away or get walked over, the fight doesn't end with bruises. It ends in reflection. How did you handle it? What did it reveal? What did it change in you?

Legacy in spirit is how you integrate the chaos. Do you grow from it? Do you stay stuck in it? Do you become bitter—or better?

Because one day, someone will ask, "What happened that night?" And how you answer will tell them who you became.

But here's what it looks like when you ignore this: You glorify the moment. You carry it like a medal instead of a mirror. You stay defined by the damage, never learning the lesson. And you keep finding new fights—because you never closed the last one.

End of Chapter Reflection: The Sidewalk Truth

It's 2:13 AM. You're outside a bar. Voices get loud. A guy bumps your shoulder, hard. He steps in. You feel the heat in your chest, the tightening in your jaw.

This is it.

You remember Rule 1—check your ego. This isn't worth it. You position your body (Rule 5), speak with calm (Rule 3), and give him space to walk away. He doesn't.

He swings.

You move. Not with rage, but with control (Rule 2). You deflect. He slips. You don't finish him. You breathe, step back, speak clearly. Others step in. It's over. You didn't lose. You didn't escalate. You didn't turn it into a viral moment for the wrong reasons.

Later, your friend says, "You handled that like a pro." You nod. But what you're really thinking is: *I trained for this moment for years, and I'm glad I never stopped.*

Fights don't define you.

How you handle them does.

ORANGE BELT

CHAPTER 3

RULES IN A COMPETITION MATCH

(THEY DIDN'T TELL YOU ABOUT)

"You don't rise to the occasion. You fall to your level of training." – Archilochus

"The fight is won or lost far away from witnesses— in the gym, behind the lines, in the ring, and out there on the road." – Muhammad Ali

Introduction

The competition mat is a strange place. It's loud but isolating. Energizing but terrifying. All eyes are on you, but none of them can help you. The bell rings, the timer starts, and suddenly, it's just you, your opponent, and the sum total of your preparation.

Competing is about more than just skill. It reveals everything— the cracks in your discipline, the truth about your ego, and the quality of your mental preparation. That's why some of the most essential life lessons aren't learned in training—they're learned under pressure, when something is actually on the line.

Here are the nine rules no one explained to you about competition—but every veteran understands.

1. Your nerves don't mean you're weak—they mean you care. *(Humility)*

Everyone gets nervous. Even champions. What separates them is not the absence of nerves—it's their relationship with them. Competition has a way of exposing all the places you've tied your self-worth to victory. Humility is understanding that being nervous doesn't mean you're not ready—it means you respect the stakes.

A humble competitor doesn't try to act cool to hide fear. They acknowledge it, breathe through it, and move anyway. They don't see competition as a chance to prove their value—just an opportunity to express their training.

But here's what it looks like when you ignore this: You pretend you're not nervous, but your body knows better. You act cocky. You underestimate your opponent. And when the nerves hit mid-match, you crumble—because you didn't respect them in advance.

2. You don't win the day of—you win weeks before. *(Discipline)*

The match starts long before the first whistle. It starts in your training. In the food you ate. The sleep you got. The reps you didn't skip. In competition, you fall to the level of your discipline—not your dreams.

The disciplined athlete makes fewer excuses. They don't panic when the match gets messy because they've already trained through worse. Their baseline effort is built, not borrowed. And win or lose, they know they brought their best.

But here's what it looks like when you ignore this: You train inconsistently. You blow off conditioning. You rely on talent instead of habit. And when the match gets tough—you fade. Not because you're untalented, but because you never practiced suffering.

3. Courage is committing to your game plan, even under fire. *(Courage)*

In a match, the pressure to abandon your game plan is massive. One bad exchange and doubt creeps in. You start reacting instead of responding. Courage isn't about throwing haymakers—it's about sticking to what you trained, even when your confidence wavers.

A courageous competitor trusts their preparation. They don't let a rough start dictate their finish. They stay calm, stay sharp, and keep chasing their win condition.

But here's what it looks like when you ignore this: You panic after one takedown. You scrap your strategy. You chase submissions that aren't there or defend desperately instead of adjusting. And you leave the mat asking, "Why didn't I just do what I trained to do?"

4. You're not fighting your opponent—you're fighting your ego. *(Ego)*

Your opponent isn't the enemy—your ego is. The voice that says, "You can't lose to this guy." Or "You've got to win to be respected." That voice pushes you to overreach, show off, or win fast.

Ego makes you believe every match defines you. That every spectator matters. But ego doesn't win matches—composure does. And when you drop the performance and embrace the moment, you fight freer, smarter, and better.

But here's what it looks like when you ignore this: You make dumb decisions to impress. You rush. You forget the technique. You tap to pride instead of pressure. And the loss stings more because it wasn't about ability—it was about ego running the show.

5. Control the pace, or the pace controls you. *(Control)*

Competition is about rhythm. If you're not setting the pace, you're chasing it. Controlling the match isn't just physical—it's mental. It's breathing when they're rushing. It's framing before flailing. It's advancing when they stall.

Controlled fighters don't need chaos. They create pressure without panic. And they never let an opponent dictate their reaction.

But here's what it looks like when you ignore this: You react to everything. You gas out trying to keep up. You fall into their game. You fight their fight. And when the clock runs out, you realize—you never took control. You just survived.

6. If you tap, own it. If you win, stay humble. *(Responsibility)*

Competition doesn't define your worth, but it does define your character. How you win and how you lose matter. Responsibility means owning both outcomes with the same class.

Win? Shake hands. Celebrate without gloating. Lose? Nod. Learn. Get better. What you show on the mat is only half the picture. What happens after the handshake is the real test.

But here's what it looks like when you ignore this: You throw your belt. You storm off. You rub your win in someone's face. You show that, for all your training, you're still emotionally immature. And that ruins even the most impressive performance.

7. Repetition creates instinct. *(Mastery)*

In a match, you don't think—you act. And what comes out under stress is whatever you drilled the most. That's why mastery matters. It's not about having 1,000 techniques. It's about having 10 that you've done 10,000 times.

The best competitors move without thinking, because their preparation has embedded excellence into muscle memory. They aren't guessing. They're reacting with precision.

But here's what it looks like when you ignore this: You blank out. You try to remember what you learned two weeks ago. But you never repped it enough to make it automatic. So your brain fumbles, your body freezes, and the opportunity slips away.

8. Someone in the crowd will remember how you carried yourself. *(Legacy in Action)*

It might be a kid. A teammate. A stranger. But someone is watching you compete—not to see if you win, but to see *how* you win. How you walk on. How you leave. What you do after the tap.

You're writing a legacy with every match. And often, it's the quiet moments—the bow, the smile, the nod—that people remember most.

But here's what it looks like when you ignore this: You make the match about you. You showboat. You argue with refs. You forget that martial arts is about respect first. And people leave remembering your attitude, not your armbar.

9. The match ends, but the impression lasts. *(Legacy in Spirit)*

Medals collect dust. Records fade. But the way you competed— your grit, your grace, your respect—that stays. Years from now, people won't remember the score. They'll remember how you made them feel.

Whether you win or lose, your spirit echoes. Make sure it's one you're proud of.

But here's what it looks like when you ignore this: You think it's "just a match." You forget that martial arts is legacy, not just combat. And one day, when someone brings up your name—they don't smile. They wince. Because how you showed up mattered more than you thought.

End of Chapter Reflection: The Match Replay

The crowd has gone quiet. Your gear is packed. You're in the car, replaying the match.

Did you respect your nerves, or pretend you were too cool to care? (**Rule 1**)

Did your training show, or did you wish you'd done more sprints, more reps, more drills? (**Rule 2**)

Did you stick to the plan, or abandon it in a rush of fear? (**Rule 3**)

Was your ego in the driver's seat, chasing validation? (**Rule 4**)

Did you control the pace, or get dragged into someone else's storm? (**Rule 5**)

How did you act after the whistle blew? Win or lose—did you carry it with class? (**Rule 6**)

Did your body respond with instinct, or freeze without direction? (**Rule 7**)

Did you walk like someone was watching—because they were? (**Rule 8**)

And will people remember the score, or your spirit? (**Rule 9**)

The next match will come. But what you do between now and then—that's where the real victory begins.

GREEN BELT

CHAPTER 4

RULES IN WARFARE

(THEY DIDN'T TELL YOU ABOUT)

"In battle, the one who adapts is the one who survives." – Miyamoto Musashi

"The supreme art of war is to subdue the enemy without fighting." – Sun Tzu

Introduction

Warfare is a chaotic system. It's not just about strength—it's about strategy, clarity, and consequence. On the battlefield, no one cares about your intentions or feelings—only your ability to survive and protect what matters.

Most of us won't step onto an actual battlefield, but life simulates it daily: job loss, divorce, betrayal, illness, crisis. These moments feel like war—ruthless, disorienting, demanding. They don't give warnings. They just come. And they expect you to be ready.

These nine rules are drawn from combat, real and metaphorical. They've saved lives. They've saved families. They can save you from yourself when pressure closes in and everything seems to be falling apart.

This isn't about romanticizing war. It's about recognizing that life doesn't care whether you feel prepared. It will throw you into the fire. Your training—mental, emotional, and physical— is what determines whether you burn out or forge ahead.

1. You are not invincible. Act accordingly. *(Humility)*

The warrior who believes he can't be hit is already halfway to dying. Arrogance kills in combat—fast and loud. Humility keeps you alert, calculated, and alive. It reminds you to double-check your surroundings. It's the quiet voice that says, "There might be something I'm missing."

Whether on the mat, in business, or navigating heartbreak, humility is the wisdom to know you're not immune to failure. It reminds you that even with skill and preparation, things can go wrong—and they will. A humble fighter trains harder, listens more, and reacts faster because he knows he's not untouchable.

But here's what it looks like when you ignore this: You rush into situations unprepared, thinking experience will save you. You ignore red flags and underestimate your opponent. You think being loud makes you strong. Until life hits you—hard—and reminds you that confidence without caution is just recklessness wearing a uniform.

2. Keep your kit clean, your rifle ready, and your boots tied. *(Discipline)*

In combat, gear isn't a fashion statement—it's survival. A dirty rifle jams. Untied boots trip you. Discipline in warfare is about details: checking your weapon daily, rehearsing drills, securing your perimeter. Not because you expect action, but because you know it could happen at any moment.

That's life. Discipline doesn't show off. It shows up. It's not dramatic; it's deliberate. The more boring your preparation, the smoother your survival. Maintenance, routine, and reps—these build the foundation that will hold when chaos arrives.

But here's what it looks like when you ignore this: You skip the small things. You assume your tools, relationships, or body will "just work." You find out during the storm that your shelter has holes. And it's too late to patch them when the bullets are already flying.

3. Courage is moving forward when every instinct screams retreat. *(Courage)*

Combat strips away fantasy. When the fear rises—real, bone-deep fear—most people freeze. But courage is choosing to move anyway. It's not being fearless. It's being obedient to your purpose despite fear.

Real courage isn't loud. It's the quiet breath before stepping out of cover. It's running toward the explosion because some-one might be alive. In life, it's the uncomfortable phone call, the painful goodbye, the chance you take when everyone else stays safe.

But here's what it looks like when you ignore this: You wait. You overthink. You hope the problem will solve itself. But the longer you delay, the worse it gets. And eventually, retreat becomes your identity, not your strategy. You never engage, and you never evolve.

4. Bravery without calculation is just stupidity. *(Ego)*

Movies often depict soldiers rushing headfirst into battle. Real life buries them. Boldness is not bravery if it lacks strategy. Your ego wants to prove something—to be seen. But war doesn't care about your image. It cares whether you make it out.

True warriors assess before they attack. They ask: Is this necessary? Is it winnable? Will this protect my people or just boost my pride? Ego gets loud. Wisdom gets lethal.

But here's what it looks like when you ignore this: You rush in blind. You ignore support. You act alone. And when the mission fails, you blame the team, the terrain, the timing—anything but the truth: you wanted glory more than victory.

5. Secure the perimeter before you push forward. *(Control)*

Before you launch the offensive, check your flank. In war, leaving your back exposed is an invitation to die. The same principle applies to life: don't take on new challenges until your current ones are secure.

Control isn't dominance—it's readiness. It's knowing your finances, your health, and your mindset are stable before adding new stress. Don't mistake momentum for progress. You can be running straight into a trap if you're not checking your six.

But here's what it looks like when you ignore this: You expand too fast. You say yes to everything. You get ambushed by responsibilities you should've locked down. Now you're overextended, underprepared, and losing ground—fast.

6. Your teammates eat before you do. *(Responsibility)*

In the field, leaders serve. If you eat first, trust breaks. If you neglect yourself and ignore the rest, morale suffers. In life, as in war, real leadership is found in sacrifice, not spotlight.

Responsibility means being the kind of person others can rely on. You guard the line. You pull the weight. Not because it's fair, but because someone has to. You do it for them because one day, they'll do it for you.

But here's what it looks like when you ignore this: You become a liability. You take the last water bottle. You prioritize comfort over commitment. And when the team needs you, you're either absent or resented. Either way, they stop counting on you.

7. Smooth reloads beat wild bursts. *(Mastery)*

Combat isn't won by who shoots the most—it's won by who reloads the cleanest under fire. Mastery isn't flash. It's fundamentals. The soldier who trains reloads a thousand times in silence so that, under pressure, he doesn't have to think.

In life, mastery means drilling the boring stuff: communication, emotional regulation, movement, and thought patterns. Not for applause—but for survivability. When the chaos hits, you won't rise to your goal—you'll fall to your level of training.

But here's what it looks like when you ignore this: You panic. You forget the plan. You rush into action half-ready, and it shows. You fire fast and loud but miss every target. And when the clip's empty, so is your advantage.

8. No one remembers the loudest. They remember the steadiest. *(Legacy in Action)*

Anyone can make noise. But on the battlefield, you remember the one who kept his voice low, his aim steady, and his morale high. Legacy in warfare is built by those who lead through consistency—not charisma.

In life, the steady friend, parent, or teammate outlasts the superstar. You don't have to be flashy. You have to be faithful. In combat and in crisis, those who can hold the line under pressure write the story that others will remember.

But here's what it looks like when you ignore this: You flare up. You disappear. You're unreliable in stress. Your story becomes one of chaos and disappointment—not legacy. Loudness fades. Steadiness echoes.

9. If you fall here, someone else might stand later.
(Legacy in Spirit)

Not every mission ends with you walking home. In war—and in life—you might give everything and not get a reward. But legacy isn't always about what you accomplish. It's about what you inspire.

Sacrifice doesn't go unnoticed. Somewhere down the line, someone will step further because you showed how to walk that stretch. What you do under pressure, even when it costs you, becomes someone else's first step.

But here's what it looks like when you ignore this: You think it's only about you. You fight short-term battles with no eye for impact. And when you fall, nothing grows behind you. The line ends with you, instead of launching from you.

End of Chapter Reflection: The Combat Scenario

Picture this:

You're deep in hostile territory. Communication is down. You and your team are cut off. Air support might not come. It's cold. It's dark. And the enemy is moving.

The youngest soldier—new and panicked—starts losing it. He looks at you.

You don't flinch.

You check your rifle. You scan the tree line. You speak low, calm, and clear. You hand out rations before taking your own. You double-check the flank, reload smoothly, and make a silent plan.

Because you knew this moment was coming. You trained for it. Not for recognition—but for survival. For them.

You didn't think you were invincible (**Rule 1**). You checked your gear, your heart, and your team before it all began (**Rule 2**). You stepped forward despite the fear (**Rule 3**). You didn't act recklessly—you acted wisely (**Rule 4**).

You covered your six before you made the call to move (**Rule 5**). You made sure they ate first (**Rule 6**). You didn't panic during the reload—you practiced for this (**Rule 7**).

They'll forget your speeches. But they'll never forget how steady you were (**Rule 8**). And if you fall—God forbid—they'll carry your legacy forward because they learned what leadership under fire looks like (**Rule 9**).

That's warfare.
That's life.
And you just made it through.

PURPLE BELT

CHAPTER 5

RULES IN CHANGING A TIRE

(THEY DIDN'T TELL YOU ABOUT)

"You can't stop the waves, but you can learn to surf." –
Jon Kabat-Zinn

"No man ever steps in the same river twice, for it's not the
same river and he's not the same man." – Heraclitus

Introduction

It's never just about the tire.

Flat tires don't happen on good days. They happen when you're running late, it's raining, your phone's dying, and there's no shoulder on the road. But that's life, isn't it? Inconvenience is rarely convenient.

Changing a tire is one of those moments where pressure, preparation, and mindset collide. You either fall apart—or rise up. But here's the real point: the flat isn't the problem. The moment is.

These aren't just tips for fixing rubber. They're rules for handling life's messes with humility, clarity, and grit. They're reminders that discomfort doesn't build character—it reveals it.

So here's what changing a tire can teach you about everything else.

1. Admit you don't know everything before it costs you. *(Humility)*

You can fake confidence until it leaves you stranded. You can bluff your way through YouTube tutorials. But when you're on the side of the road, none of that matters if you don't have a jack—or know how to use one.

Humility isn't saying, "I'm useless." It's saying, "I don't know this yet, and I need help or preparation." That admission might mean learning before the crisis hits. It might mean calling someone instead of pretending. It might mean swallowing pride to ask a stranger.

Smart people still get flats. Humble people don't turn them into disasters.

But here's what it looks like when you ignore this: You act like you've got it handled. You refuse help. You break bolts, forget steps, or stare at a manual in denial while your pride digs you deeper. The flat isn't what stalls you—ego is. And every minute wasted pretending adds up to hours you didn't need to lose.

2. Do the maintenance before the breakdown. *(Discipline)*

Discipline is what you do before it matters. It's recommended to check the tire pressure monthly. It's making sure the spare has air. It's keeping the jack where it belongs. These small, mundane acts may seem unnecessary—until they save the day.

The same applies to your health, relationships, and finances. If you wait until the crisis, you're already late. Preparedness isn't glamorous, but it's what separates chaos from control.

Real discipline happens long before the tire goes flat.

But here's what it looks like when you ignore this: You assume you'll deal with it when the time comes. You haven't checked your kit in years. You don't even know if there's a spare in the trunk. And when the tire blows? Panic. Regret. Delays. Suddenly, every previously ignored detail becomes the difference between being stuck and being safe.

3. It's okay to be rattled, but act anyway. *(Courage)*

Nobody feels heroic next to a busted tire in the rain. You're cold. Frustrated. Embarrassed. Cars are flying past. And inside, part of you wants to wait for someone else to fix it.

But courage isn't bravado. It's a quiet action. It's reaching for the wrench even when your hands shake. It's doing what needs to be done, not because it feels good, but because it's the next right thing.

Fear is normal. What you do next defines you.

But here's what it looks like when you ignore this: You freeze. You overthink. You keep checking your phone, hoping a miracle will arrive. But help doesn't always come. And while you wait for certainty, the rain keeps falling and the problem stays unsolved. Courage is built in moments like this—uncomfortable, unchosen, but undeniable.

4. Your ego doesn't tighten bolts. *(Ego)*

It's raining. You're covered in grime. And maybe people are watching. So what? This isn't the time for vanity.

Ego tells you you're above this—that you shouldn't have to deal with it. But ego doesn't change tires. It doesn't get you home. What does? Willingness. Humility. Focus—the readiness to kneel in the dirt and get it done.

Ask for help. Use the manual. Learn something new. There's no shame in not knowing—only in refusing to.

But here's what it looks like when you ignore this: You try to "tough it out" to impress someone. You dismiss advice. You pretend everything's under control while the situation worsens. And afterward, instead of a simple fix, you're left with damage, wasted time, and a bruised ego that accomplished nothing.

5. Slow is smooth. Smooth is fast. *(Control)*

The fastest way to screw up a tire change is to rush. Skip a step. Over-tighten a lug nut. Forget to block the wheels. Suddenly, your car's rolling, or your wheel's warped—or worse.

Control means slowing down to speed up. It's taking a breath before the next step. It's following the process, even when the clock says panic. Smoothness saves time in the long run—and preserves safety.

Control isn't about force. It's about flow.

But here's what it looks like when you ignore this: You rush. You miss a step. You twist bolts wrong and make the next fix harder. Or worse—you get back on the road with something dangerously loose. Rushing might feel productive, but control is what keeps you alive.

6. Someone else might need your calm. *(Responsibility)*

Maybe your kid's in the back seat. Maybe a partner's panicking. Maybe a stranger pulled over to help. Whoever's nearby—they're watching you.

Your energy sets the tone. Panic multiplies. Calm diffuses. Responsibility here isn't just about changing a tire—it's about leadership in tension. Stay grounded. Speak clearly. Move with intent.

Even if no one's watching, you're still teaching yourself who you become under pressure.

But here's what it looks like when you ignore this: You curse. You slam tools. You let frustration turn into chaos. And suddenly, a teachable moment becomes trauma. Your kids learn to fear stress. Your partner sees volatility, not stability. Your reaction teaches more than the situation ever could.

7. Know your tools inside and out. *(Mastery)*

It's one thing to own a jack. It's another to know exactly where it fits, how it lifts, and what to do when something goes wrong. Mastery is in the muscle memory—the rehearsed, repeated, refined skill that shows up when it matters most.

This isn't just about tools. It's about knowledge. Practice. Intimacy with your craft. When crisis hits, the time for learning is over—the time for execution begins.

But here's what it looks like when you ignore this: You fumble with the jack. You tighten bolts backwards. You get halfway through before realizing you missed a step. You have the tools—but not the training. And that gap becomes the space where mistakes happen.

8. Someone taught you how to do this. Pass it on. *(Legacy in Action)*

You didn't invent tire-changing. Someone showed you. A parent. A friend. A stranger. A YouTube video. That gift—a few minutes of knowledge—saved you hours of pain. Now it's your turn.

Legacy isn't grand speeches. It's teaching someone how to handle life with capability and calm. Pay it forward. Let someone watch. Let someone learn.

One act of guidance can have a lasting impact that ripples through generations.

But here's what it looks like when you ignore this: You fix it. Drive off. And the next person breaks down with no idea what to do. You had a chance to make someone else's life easier, and you stayed silent. You hoarded what was meant to be passed on.

9. Long after the tires changed, the lesson stays.
(Legacy in Spirit)

You won't remember every detail. But you'll remember how you felt: steady or frantic, confident or lost. And whoever watched you—your child, a stranger, your future self—will remember it too.

That's legacy. It's not the action. It's the energy. The example. The silent story you told through your choices.

These moments echo. Let the echo build someone stronger.

But here's what it looks like when you ignore this: You treat it like a chore. You miss the metaphor. You rush away, thinking it doesn't matter. But every moment teaches something. Even a flat tire. Especially a flat tire.

End of Chapter Reflection: The Tire Change

You're pulled over. Hazard lights are blinking. Rain tapping the roof. Your phone's almost dead, and you're already late. In the backseat, your kid watches silently. You glance in the rearview mirror and see fear in their eyes.

You breathe.

You open the trunk. The spare's ready. So is the kit. Not perfect—but enough. You crouch. Loosen bolts. Lift the car. Swap the tire. Your hands are cold. Your knees are muddy. But you keep moving.

You didn't panic (**Rule 1**). You'd prepped for this (**Rule 2**). You acted anyway, despite the frustration (**Rule 3**). You asked for help when needed and didn't pretend to know it all (**Rule 4**).

You moved slowly, steadily (**Rule 5**). You stayed calm for your child (**Rule 6**). You knew exactly how the jack worked (**Rule 7**). And after, you opened the door and said, "Let me show you how I did that." (**Rule 8**)

They'll never forget it. And neither will you. (**Rule 9**)

BLUE BELT

CHAPTER 6

RULES IN A BREAKUP

(THEY DIDN'T TELL YOU ABOUT)

*"The wound is the place where the
Light enters you." – Rumi*

*"We suffer more often in imagination
than in reality." – Seneca*

Introduction

Breakups don't just end relationships. They shatter routines, rewrite futures, and reveal truths we tried to ignore. Whether it was your decision or theirs—whether the breakup was clean or chaotic—breakups expose the rawest parts of us. They challenge our identity, our self-worth, and our stability. But beneath the pain, there's a pattern. Beneath the collapse, there's a curriculum.

This isn't just about romance. It's about detachment, transformation, and rebuilding. It's about losing what felt like a piece of yourself and realizing you were always whole.

Like the mat, the fight, or the flat tire—there are rules. Unwritten, unseen, but undeniable once you've walked through the wreckage. Here are the ones I wish someone had told me sooner.

1. You're not less because they left. *(Humility)*

Breakups are identity earthquakes. They rattle your core, distort your reflection, and tempt you to believe you're suddenly less than you were. But here's the truth: someone leaving does not subtract from your value. Their departure isn't an invoice on your worth. Humility in heartbreak means facing your flaws without forfeiting your self-respect.

Maybe you showed up poorly. Own it. Perhaps you gave your all, and it still didn't work out. Respect it. Either way, humility is the strength to look in the mirror and see both what needs growth and what deserves grace. This isn't about beating yourself up—it's about being honest, grounded, and real. You're still whole, even if you feel hollow.

But here's what it looks like when you ignore this: You beg for validation. You chase their attention. You scroll through old texts like scripture, hoping for a different ending. You let their silence define your narrative. And in that obsession, you forget that your value isn't up for negotiation. You lose twice—once in the breakup, and again in your identity.

2. Don't skip the process. *(Discipline)*

There's no shortcut through a breakup. You can't speedrun grief or fake closure. Healing is slow, uneven, and often dull. Discipline in this context doesn't look like strict routines—it looks like showing up for yourself when you'd rather not.

Feel it. Journal it. Train through it. Do the things that restore your strength and your spirit, even if they don't make the pain disappear immediately. Discipline is about choosing structure in the chaos, opting for nourishment over numbing, and cultivating habits that rebuild.

You may want to run. To distract. But healing isn't avoidance—it's endurance.

But here's what it looks like when you ignore this: You jump into another relationship to prove you're over it. You numb out with social media, substances, or busyness. You keep looking for something to fill the space they left. But the pain doesn't go—it buries itself. And when it resurfaces, it demands to be felt all over again. The discipline you skip today becomes the damage you carry tomorrow.

3. It takes courage to sit with heartbreak. *(Courage)*

Courage in a breakup isn't about dramatic gestures. It's not about begging or burning bridges. It's about silence. Stillness. Staying in your lane while the dust settles.

It's resisting the urge to message them. It's sitting in a quiet room with nothing but your grief and your breath. Courage is in the patience to heal before you perform. It's allowing the space to miss someone without rushing to replace them. And it's the bravery to move forward without needing to prove you're okay before you actually are.

But here's what it looks like when you ignore this: You chase ghosts. You send late-night texts hoping for clarity. You post for attention instead of expression. You confuse noise for progress. But courage doesn't live in the reaction—it lives in the restraint. And every time you break that stillness, you set your healing back another step.

4. Don't fight to prove your worth. *(Ego)*

After a breakup, your ego kicks into overdrive. It wants revenge. It wants them to see you "thriving." But healing isn't performance. It's reconstruction. You don't need to "win" the breakup. You need to recover your truth, your peace, your power.

Your value isn't up for review. If you're still living for their opinion, then they're still in control. Let go of the stage. Let go of the scoreboard. Let go of the need to be seen succeeding by the person who hurt you.

But here's what it looks like when you ignore this: You curate your feed like a highlight reel. You flaunt your "glow up" for their attention. But behind the filters and the flexing, the ache lingers. You're not healing—you're campaigning. And ego doesn't rebuild. It just distracts from the truth: this pain isn't fixed by being admired. It's fixed by being honest.

5. Control what's in your hands. *(Control)*

You cannot control what they feel, what they say, or what story they tell others. You can't rewrite their narrative, and trying to only makes you feel more powerless.

What you can control is your reaction. Your routine. Your habits. You can choose how you show up to work, how you treat your body, and how you speak about them when they're not around.

Control starts at the edge of your own behavior—and that's more than enough.

But here's what it looks like when you ignore this: You spiral. You obsess. You stalk their updates, trying to decode meaning from emojis. You burn hours trying to win a game you're no longer playing. But all the energy you spend on them is energy stolen from your rebuild. Control is not about them. It's about you reclaiming your peace.

6. If you said you loved them, act like it—even in goodbye. *(Responsibility)*

Love doesn't end with possession. Sometimes, the most loving thing you can do is to let go—without bitterness, without blame. If you meant what you said when you were together, honor it in how you separate.

This doesn't mean staying in touch. It means carrying yourself with the kind of integrity you would want modeled for someone you cared about. Responsibility in a breakup is grace under emotional fire.

But here's what it looks like when you ignore this: You gossip. You vent on social media. You expose their secrets out of spite. You turn the ending into a war zone. And all it proves is that the love was conditional, dependent on staying. But love, real love, leaves the door closed gently—even when it hurts.

7. Reflect, don't rehearse. *(Mastery)*

Mastery isn't about erasing pain—it's about learning from it. Reflecting means asking: what patterns did I repeat? What wounds did I ignore? What role did I play?

Rehearsing, on the other hand, is a trap. It's replaying old fights in your head. It's imagining comebacks you'll never say. It's indulging in the fantasy of "what if."

To master a loss is to extract meaning, not to relive the moments. Growth doesn't live in loops. It lives in insight.

But here's what it looks like when you ignore this: You get stuck. You treat pain like a stage play. Same scenes. Same roles. Same audience as one. And while your mind rehearses the drama, your life stays on pause. Reflection is movement. Rehearsal is stagnation.

8. You are someone's example of how to lose with honor. *(Legacy in Action)*

Someone is watching how you handle this. A sibling. A friend. Your child. A future partner. The way you carry yourself through the storm becomes a blueprint for others.

Legacy doesn't start when you "win." It begins when you show dignity in defeat. Let your posture say, "This hurts, but I won't collapse." Be the proof that pain doesn't have to be poison.

But here's what it looks like when you ignore this: You let your pain bleed everywhere. You teach others that bitterness is typical, that revenge is justified, and that heartbreak excuses harm. But your example—intentional or not—will echo. The question is: will it echo strength or spite?

9. The people you've loved shape the way you love next. *(Legacy in Spirit)*

Even when they're gone, they leave marks. In your trust. In your defenses. In your empathy. That person—whether they loved you well or poorly—becomes a thread in the fabric of who you are.

You don't forget them. But you can choose what their memory teaches you. Will it close you off—or open you up with wisdom?

This is legacy in spirit: letting your past refine your future, not define it.

But here's what it looks like when you ignore this: You shut down. You armor up. You make the next person pay for the one before. But all that does is let the ghost of a past love dictate your future. And nothing about that is strength.

End of Chapter Reflection: The Message You Never Sent

You sit on the edge of your bed. Phone in hand. Heart pounding. There's a message typed out—but unsent. You've reworded it a dozen times.

"I miss you."

"You hurt me."

"I just want closure."

But this time, you delete it.

Not because you're stone-hearted. Not because you stopped caring. But because you finally realize the message isn't for them. It's for you.

You admit the wound without needing it validated (**Rule 1**). You didn't run to distraction—you chose stillness (**Rule 2**). You resisted the urge to perform your pain for an audience that no longer matters (**Rule 3**).

You let your ego rest. You chose peace over points (**Rule 4**). You cleaned your space, hit the gym, and did the work that actually moves you forward (**Rule 5**).

You didn't lash out. You honored your past by ending with integrity (**Rule 6**). You journaled the patterns, not the poison (**Rule 7**).

Later, someone says, "You handled that with grace." And you smile—not because it didn't hurt, but because you didn't break. You became someone worth remembering (**Rules 8 & 9**).

BROWN
BELT

CHAPTER 7

RULES IN RAISING A CHILD

(THEY DIDN'T TELL YOU ABOUT)

"Children are educated by what the grown-up is and not by his talk." – Carl Jung

"Give me a child until he is 7 and I will show you the man." – Aristotle

Introduction

Raising a child is more complicated than any fight, belt test, or board break. There's no warmup, no clear grading system, and no applause at the end of each day. You don't earn parenting stripes—you carry them silently, in fatigue, worry, and hope.

But every day you show up, you teach them something, not by your speeches, but by your behavior. **You are the curriculum.** What you tolerate, how you respond, how you love, and how you lead—all of it becomes their template.

Parenting isn't about creating perfect children. It's about becoming the kind of adult you hope they one day become.

These are the rules I wish more parents lived by—because children don't forget how we make them feel.

1. Show them how to lose first. *(Humility)*

Your child will face failure. That's guaranteed. The question is: **what have you taught them about it?** Have they seen you fail with composure? Have they heard you apologize? Have they watched you get up after falling?

Humility in parenting is modeling grace, not dominance. Let them see your cracks. Show them that strength isn't in pretending—it's in honesty. When you say, "I was wrong," you teach them that being human is not the same as being weak.

But here's what it looks like when you ignore this: You always need to win the argument. You can't say sorry. You hide mistakes. And your kids grow up thinking failure means shame. That perfection is the standard. And when they fall—they break, because they never saw how to bend.

2. Teach them through routine. *(Discipline)*

Discipline isn't punishment. It's pattern. The power of repetition, boundaries, and consistency can't be overstated. It builds safety. It builds trust. And it builds resilience.

Kids thrive in structure. They push against it—not because they hate it, but because they need to know it's solid. Regular bedtimes. Scheduled meals. Consequences that match behavior. That's how you teach not just behavior—but identity.

Discipline becomes the inner voice they hear when life gets noisy.

But here's what it looks like when you ignore this: You parent by mood. You threaten more than you follow through. You let tiredness become an excuse for inconsistency. And over time, your kids learn that rules are negotiable—and safety is uncertain.

3. Let them try, even if they fall. *(Courage)*

You can't shield your child from the world. And the more you try, the more you stunt their growth. Courage isn't built in bubble wrap—it's built in bruises.

Let them attempt the hard thing. Let them stumble. Let them feel frustration. And then guide them. Catch them when they fall—but don't stop them from falling.

Be the net, not the leash.

But here's what it looks like when you ignore this: You micromanage. You rescue too early. You rob them of small struggles—and with it, small victories. So, when a real challenge comes? They're frozen. Uncertain. Fragile. Because they were never allowed to become strong.

4. Your child is not your trophy. *(Ego)*

They are not your second chance. They're not your redemption arc or brand extension. They're not here to make you look good on social media or fulfill the dreams you abandoned.

They are their own person. And your job is to see them clearly, **not project yourself onto them**.

Support them. Challenge them. But let them grow into *who they are*.

But here's what it looks like when you ignore this: You push too hard. You brag too much. You correct in public to save face. You dismiss their interests in favor of yours. And they grow up confused about who they are, because they were never allowed to become anything else.

5. Create calm—they'll mirror it. *(Control)*

Kids don't need you to be calm all the time. But they need to see that emotions can be **felt without being weaponized.** Your regulation becomes their model.

When things get tense, when they scream, when they cry—how do you respond? Do you escalate? Or do you ground? Do you show them what self-control looks like?

Breathe first. Speak second. Let calm be your leadership style.

But here's what it looks like when you ignore this: You yell. You slam doors. You explode. And then you apologize, but the pattern sticks. Your kids learn that chaos is a form of power. That loud wins. And when they grow up, they don't regulate—they repeat.

6. What you tolerate teaches them what's acceptable. *(Responsibility)*

Boundaries are love in action. Every time you correct disrespect, reinforce kindness, or stop bad habits, you're shaping future behavior.

What you ignore becomes permission. What you accept becomes belief.

You're not just raising a child. You're shaping someone's partner, leader, employee, or coach. Teach with that weight in mind.

But here's what it looks like when you ignore this: You let rudeness slide because you're tired. You reward bad behavior with attention. You ignore your own rules. And your kids learn: everything is negotiable, and consequences are just suggestions.

7. Repetition is their curriculum. *(Mastery)*

Kids don't learn by hearing it once. Or twice. Or five times. They learn by living it daily. And you'll repeat yourself so many times you feel like a broken record. That's normal.

Mastery in childhood isn't about speed—it's about saturation. Repeat, reinforce, recalibrate. And eventually, it sticks.

Be patient. Be consistent. Be their guide, not their critic.

But here's what it looks like when you ignore this: You get impatient. You call them "bad listeners." You label them instead of leading them. And instead of learning, they shrink. Repetition isn't failure—it's how their brain wires success.

8. Your example outlasts your instructions.
(Legacy in Action)

They won't remember all your speeches. But they'll remember how you handled stress. How you talked to the waiter. How you treated them when you were angry.

Your behavior becomes their blueprint for adulthood. So when you think no one's watching—they are. **And they're learning.**

Live the standard you want them to carry.

But here's what it looks like when you ignore this: You say "be kind" but gossip at dinner. You say "be responsible" but blame everyone else. And your kids stop trusting your words— because your actions speak louder.

9. One day, they'll raise someone just like you.
(Legacy in Spirit)

The final test of parenting isn't how your kids treat *you*—it's how they treat their own children. Because what you model will echo.

How you spoke. How you loved. How you led. It gets passed on—quietly, unconsciously, powerfully.

You're not just raising a child. You're shaping a lineage.

But here's what it looks like when you ignore this: You act like parenting ends at 18. You forget that habits outlive hugs. And your unspoken legacy—good or bad—becomes the standard your grandkids will experience secondhand.

End of Chapter Reflection: The Kitchen Table

It's dinner time. The table is cluttered. The food is simple. The day was long.

Your kid asks a question—hard, honest, maybe even scary. You pause. You don't deflect. You answer, fully present. You don't lecture. You connect.

They saw you apologize earlier (**Rule 1**). They knew dinner would be at 6, like always (**Rule 2**). They spilled water, cleaned it up themselves, and you thanked them (**Rule 3**). You praised their effort, not their performance (**Rule 4**).

They heard your tone stay calm when your partner got upset (**Rule 5**). They watched you correct their sarcasm—not with shame, but with truth (**Rule 6**).

You read the same book for the fifth night in a row (**Rule 7**). You hugged them before bed, and they felt safe. Not because of what you said, but because of who you were (**Rule 8**).

And years from now, when they're at their own kitchen table, they'll do the same—because you taught them how. Not by command. But by example. (**Rule 9**)

BLACK
BELT

CHAPTER 8
RULES WHEN YOU'RE LOSING
(THEY DIDN'T TELL YOU ABOUT)

"Man is not worried by real problems so much as by his imagined anxieties about real problems." – Epictetus

"Rock bottom became the solid foundation on which I rebuilt my life." – J.K. Rowling

Introduction

Losing doesn't always come with a warning. Sometimes, it's slow—unfolding like fog. Sometimes it's sudden—a cut, a collapse, a punch in the gut. But no matter how it hits you, **loss strips you down**. It reveals who you are, stripped of the scoreboard, the title, and the applause.

You learn more in the valleys than on the peaks. Pain has a way of showing you the parts of yourself that comfort never could. And while the world worships winners, it's how you lose that builds your legacy.

This chapter isn't about fixing it. It's about **facing it**. These are the rules no one tells you when everything starts to fall apart—but they're the ones you'll need most when you do.

1. Admit when you're down, and get up anyway. *(Humility)*

There's nothing noble about denial. Saying "I'm fine" when you're not only delays the comeback. Losing doesn't make you weak. It makes you honest. Humility is what lets you stop pretending and start healing.

You have to call it what it is: a setback. Not a sentence. A loss. Not a label. This is the hard reset—the truth you have to say out loud before anything else works. From there, you stand. Slowly. Quietly. But you stand.

But here's what it looks like when you ignore this: You bluff your way through it. You hide behind productivity, humor, distraction. You deny the fall until you're too tired to climb out. And no one can help—because no one knows you need it.

2. Stick to the plan even when the scoreboard says quit. *(Discipline)*

Discipline is easy when you're winning. It's when you're losing that it actually matters. Can you still show up? Still lift? Still write? Still train?

Loss tricks you into believing your actions don't matter. But they do. Maybe now more than ever. When everything feels pointless, routine becomes your rope. It's the lifeline that keeps you anchored when the waves come.

Do the reps. Follow the plan. Not for results, but for identity.

But here's what it looks like when you ignore this: You give up. You ghost your goals. You say "what's the point?" and let go of the only thing still holding you together. And when you quit the routine, you lose more than momentum—you lose yourself.

3. Courage isn't winning—it's not walking away when you're behind. *(Courage)*

The world celebrates comebacks—but forgets the quiet courage it takes to **stay** in the fight long before the victory. There's bravery in continuing when you're behind, unseen, and exhausted.

Sometimes, courage is just **showing up** again: to the meeting, to the mat, to your own reflection. It's not about pretending you're not hurt. It's about refusing to bow out because you are.

Courage is consistency in chaos.

But here's what it looks like when you ignore this: You stop answering calls. You skip training. You let the silence swallow you. You wait for a spark, a sign, a moment—when the real signal was your choice to keep going without one.

4. Don't let your pride be louder than your learning. *(Ego)*

Everyone wants to blame the loss on something else: bad luck, a cheap shot, a biased call. But that won't teach you anything.

Losing is painful—but it's also data. It shows you where to adjust, where to grow. If your pride drowns out the feedback, you'll lose again, bigger.

Ego protects your image. But it also keeps you stuck. Let it die so you can evolve.

But here's what it looks like when you ignore this: You make excuses. You defend instead of evaluate. And each time you avoid the truth, you give more power to the version of you that *failed*, instead of the one trying to rise.

5. Reset your breathing. Regain control. *(Control)*

When everything feels like it's spinning, start with your breath. It's the first thing panic steals—and the first thing that brings you back.

Inhale. Hold. Exhale. Again.

Control isn't about outcomes—it's about response. When you breathe, you lower the noise. And in that silence, clarity returns. It's not magic. It's mechanics. Your body follows your breath.

But here's what it looks like when you ignore this: You snap. You spiral. You drown in overanalysis. You say and do things you regret. And afterward, you call it "stress"—but it was actually just unregulated chaos. Your breath was the answer the whole time.

6. The people who support you when you lose are your real team. *(Responsibility)*

When you win, the crowd comes alive. When you lose, the real ones come close. That's your team. That's your tribe.

They don't cheer because of what you achieve—they stand beside you because of who you are. And part of your responsibility now is to recognize, honor, and protect those bonds.

Show up for them. Be there even when you're empty. Let loyalty be your legacy.

But here's what it looks like when you ignore this: You isolate. You pull away. You assume they wouldn't understand. But in doing so, you starve the connection that could've been your strength. And you teach yourself that support isn't real, even though it is.

7. Study the loss like you'd study your opponent. *(Mastery)*

A loss is not a failure—it's film. Watch it. Analyze it. Break it down like a competitor. What did you miss? What did you do well? What did you repeat?

Mastery comes from treating the loss with curiosity, not shame. You don't have to like the pain. But you should respect the lesson. Because the only thing worse than losing **is losing the same way again**.

But here's what it looks like when you ignore this: You pretend it didn't happen. You move on too fast. You bury it under bravado or distraction. And the pattern repeats—because the feedback was there, but you refused to hear it.

8. How you lose is part of your legacy.
(Legacy in Action)

Everyone sees how you win. But how you lose? That's what people remember.

Do you storm off? Do you own it? Do you show up the next day with your head high and your ego low?

Your legacy isn't just about success—it's about composure under fire. About what you model when nothing is going your way.

But here's what it looks like when you ignore this: You quit publicly. You rage. You run. You make the moment about emotion, not evolution. And the people watching—especially the ones who look up to you—learn that failure is final, not formative.

9. One day, someone else will face the same fall—and remember how you stood back up.
(Legacy in Spirit)

Your story matters more than you think. Someone—now or years from now—is going to hit the same wall. And when they do, they'll think of you.

They'll remember that you didn't disappear. That you didn't self-destruct. That you stood up. Quietly. Consistently.

You're writing the blueprint for someone else's resilience.

But here's what it looks like when you ignore this: You disappear. You ghost your community. You stop trying—and someone close to you watches that collapse and assumes it's normal. You never meant to teach them that—but you did.

End of Chapter Reflection: The Empty Gym

It's late. The lights buzz overhead. You're in the gym. Alone.

No music. No coach. Just the bar, the bag, or the mat—and your own heartbeat.

You lost today. Badly. Maybe in a match. Maybe in your career. Maybe in your mind. You came back anyway.

You admitted the hit hurt (**Rule 1**). You followed the plan, even though it felt pointless (**Rule 2**). You pressed record on the camera and kept going, without an audience (**Rule 3**).

You reviewed the tape, dropped the excuses, and took notes (**Rule 4**). You inhaled until your hands stopped shaking (**Rule 5**).

You replied to the friend who checked in (**Rule 6**). You watched the tape again. This time slower. You rewrote the game plan (**Rule 7**).

And tomorrow, when you walk back into that room, someone will notice. A student. A peer. A stranger. They'll see how you held your loss. And it will shift something in them too (**Rules 8 & 9**).

You didn't win. But you grew. And that? That's the beginning of something unbreakable.

RED & BLACK BELT

CHAPTER 9

RULES WHEN YOU THINK YOU'VE LOST EVERYTHING

(THEY DIDN'T TELL YOU ABOUT)

"He who has a why to live can bear almost any how." – Friedrich Nietzsche

"If you're going through hell, keep going." – Winston Churchill

Introduction

Rock bottom isn't metaphorical. It's physical. It's when your chest tightens while walking into work, when the bathroom floor becomes your place of prayer, when the mirror doesn't even look like you anymore.

You lose the job, the partner, the dream, the sense of self—and suddenly it feels like everything's slipping. But it's not the end. It's the start of your real training.

This chapter is about that moment when you feel like nothing's left. It's where first-world comforts can't save you. Where motivation is useless and habits are all you have. It's where people with less have more peace, and you're left wondering why.

You're not weak. You're not broken. You're just buried. This is how you rise.

1. Say it out loud: "I'm not okay." *(Humility)*

The most critical words in recovery aren't "I've got this." They're "I'm not okay." That's not defeat—it's the first act of strength. Humility is stepping out of your own denial and into truth. You can't fix what you won't name. Say it out loud. To your spouse. To your coach. To the mirror.

You're not supposed to be bulletproof. You're supposed to be real. The more you pretend, the deeper the damage gets. But honesty cracks the shell. It lets the right people in. It allows air in—and eventually, light.

But here's what it looks like when you ignore this: You keep performing. You tell everyone you're "fine." You bury yourself under work, sarcasm, or silence. And the people who could help? They're watching a highlight reel while you're living a horror film. No one rescues a man who won't admit he's drowning.

2. Do one small thing. Then another. *(Discipline)*

Don't try to rebuild your life today. Just make your bed. Drink a glass of water. Get outside. Discipline in crisis isn't a comeback montage—it's movement. When everything feels impossible, pick one small thing and do it without emotion. Just do it.

That's how you begin again. You make one right decision, then another. You don't trust feelings right now. You trust action. It's not exciting. It's not heroic. But it works. It rebuilds your rhythm. It repairs your dignity. And it's the first brick in a new foundation.

But here's what it looks like when you ignore this: You spiral. Days blur into each other. You binge distractions. You tell yourself you'll get it together "tomorrow." But there is no tomorrow when you're numb. There's only right now—and what you choose to do with it.

3. Stand up even when you don't believe you can. *(Courage)*

The comeback isn't one big speech. It's not a single moment of triumph. It's quiet. Lonely. Often invisible. It's choosing to keep going before the breakthrough, before the hope, before anything feels better.

That's real courage.

It's going to work with tears still drying. It's showing up for your kids when you feel like you're failing. It's getting under the bar when your chest still feels heavy from everything else.

You keep walking—not because you feel brave, but because you remember that standing still will break you even more.

But here's what it looks like when you ignore this: You retreat. You cancel plans. You disappear into digital distractions and tell yourself no one would notice. But someone would—*you* would. Every time you abandon yourself, you teach your nervous system to stay down instead of rise.

4. You're not entitled to ease. *(Ego)*

One of the biggest lies modern culture sells is that you shouldn't struggle. That if you're good, strong, kind, or skilled, life should be smooth. But the truth is: life doesn't owe you peace. And the moment you demand it, you lose your power.

Let go of the fantasy that your path was supposed to be easier. Hard doesn't mean wrong. It means real. When you stop resisting struggle and start embracing it, you become someone no storm can shake.

But here's what it looks like when you ignore this: You whine. You blame others. You scroll past people with less who smile more, and get bitter. But that's ego talking. Entitlement doesn't create progress. It creates pity. And pity is a prison you lock yourself in.

5. Reclaim your breath before you reclaim your plan. *(Control)*

Control doesn't start with a calendar or a checklist. It begins with breath. Deep, honest, grounding breath. When your world spins, when everything feels chaotic, pause. Inhale. Exhale. Let your system reset.

Then act.

You can't plan clearly when you're panicking. You can't rebuild while hyperventilating. The breath is the doorway back into yourself. Walk through it before you try walking back into your life.

But here's what it looks like when you ignore this: You chase solutions in a frenzy. You try to fix it all at once. But nothing sticks—because you're still mentally drowning. Breath comes first. Without it, every plan crumbles under emotional weight.

6. Let someone love you—even when you don't love yourself. *(Responsibility)*

When you're broken, connection feels unbearable. You don't want to be seen like this. But you need it. You need someone who will just sit with you in the quiet. Not fix. Just be.

Responsibility isn't just showing up for others—it's letting others show up for you. Text back. Open the door. Accept the offer. That's not weakness. That's wisdom.

But here's what it looks like when you ignore this: You're ghosting everyone. You punish the people who still care. You confuse isolation with independence. But you're not proving strength—you're guaranteeing more pain. Connection is medicine. Don't spit it out.

7. Journal it. Speak it. Break the loop. *(Mastery)*

Pain unspoken becomes poison. Your brain will loop the same memory, the same fear, until it becomes a groove so deep you can't climb out. Journaling breaks the cycle. Speaking drains the pressure.

Mastery here doesn't mean solutions. It means *naming* the pattern. Because once you name it, you can change it.

But here's what it looks like when you ignore this: You stay quiet. You lie to your therapist, to your journal, to yourself. You let your inner world stay vague and loud—and wonder why your body feels heavy. The pen is a scalpel. Use it.

8. The climb becomes your story. *(Legacy in Action)*

No one is inspired by someone who never suffered. The people who change lives are the ones who kept climbing when it felt hopeless. They become the proof.

Right now, you're writing that story. And one day, someone will be where you are now. They'll need your scars. They'll need your voice. Let your climb mean something.

But here's what it looks like when you ignore this: You pretend it didn't happen. You put your pain in a box. You walk around whole on the outside but hollow inside. And someone close to you thinks *they're* alone—because you never said you once were too.

9. The spirit survives what the body thinks it can't.
(Legacy in Spirit)

History is filled with people who had every reason to quit—and didn't. Survivors of war. Prisoners of tragedy. Children who grew up in silence and became protectors.

Why? Because the spirit isn't bound by comfort. It endures. It rises. It transforms.

You're part of that lineage now.

But here's what it looks like when you ignore this: You let despair win. You convince yourself the story's over when it was just turning. You give up not because you're weak—but because you forgot who you are. Remember now. Begin again.

End of Chapter Reflection: The Mirror

It's 2 a.m.

You're on the edge of your bed. Not because you're tired— because you're lost. The silence is loud. The future feels blank. And everything inside you whispers, "This is it. I'm done."

But you don't listen.

You get up. You drink water. You breathe. You cry. You write. You text back.

You don't rebuild your life tonight. But you start the process. One tiny choice. Then another.

You admit you're not okay (**Rule 1**). You do one task anyway (**Rule 2**). You stand even while doubting (**Rule 3**). You stop expecting fairness and embrace grit (**Rule 4**).

You take a breath before the next step (**Rule 5**). You let someone love you even when you don't feel lovable (**Rule 6**). You name the pain and release the poison (**Rule 7**).

You remember your story matters—not just to you, but to someone who hasn't climbed out yet (**Rule 8**). And you remind yourself: the spirit doesn't quit. It rises (**Rule 9**).

You didn't lose everything. You rediscovered who's been here all along.

You.

RED
BELT

CHAPTER 10

RULES IN LIFE

(THEY DIDN'T TELL YOU ABOUT)

"Know thyself." – Socrates

"The obstacle is the way." – Marcus Aurelius

Introduction

By now, you've traveled through nine chapters—each one a dojo of its own. We've been in the street, the arena, the home, the trenches of heartbreak, and the quiet chaos of fatherhood. Every place had its own pressure. Its own lessons. But through every scene, a deeper rhythm played beneath the surface.

You may not have noticed it at first, but every chapter followed the same arc—nine rules, repeated in spirit. Each one rooted in a color, a belt rank, a stage of personal evolution. That wasn't an accident.

In martial arts, the belt system isn't just about skill. It's about character. It's a metaphor for life's growth phases. From White (Humility) to Red (Spiritual Legacy), these stages reflect the internal journey of a martial artist—and, by extension, a human being.

Not all martial arts systems use the same belt colors or even the same rank structure. But one thing is universal: every journey begins with white, and for the few who persist, it culminates at black. Fewer still continue beyond that—to red.

White is innocence. Ignorance. The start of something. Black is proficiency. Commitment. A life transformed. But red? Red is something rarer. It isn't about being the best fighter—it's about becoming a steward of the art. A master of the invisible. A quiet leader.

In many systems, only one in 10,000 will reach black belt. And of those, even fewer will reach red. The journey is steep and unforgiving:

This chapter is the mirror. The unifying thread. Not new rules—but the final revelation of what those rules really were all along.

1. White Belt — Humility: Start Where You Are

The white belt is the beginning of everything. It symbolizes a blank slate, the willingness to be taught, the absence of ego. In life, this is your first rule: admit you don't know. That you're still learning. That you have blind spots, weaknesses, and work to do.

Humility isn't self-deprecation. It's clarity. It's the voice inside that says, "There's more to learn." It's what allows you to ask for help, to listen to feedback, and to admit when you're wrong. It's the foundation every other virtue is built upon.

The proud will fall. The curious will grow.

You can't climb if you think you're already at the top. Whether it's learning to change a tire, navigating heartbreak, or raising a child—humility is the entry point to growth. Start where you are, not where you wish you were.

And start with open hands, not clenched fists.

2. Yellow Belt — Discipline: Keep Going When It's Boring

Discipline is the quiet commitment. No spotlights. No applause. Just repetition in the dark.

At Yellow Belt, the student is no longer brand new—but far from mastery. And that's where most people quit. Because discipline isn't exciting. It's not a breakthrough or a highlight reel. It's brushing your teeth. Returning to the gym. Having the hard conversation. Showing up when you don't feel like it.

Discipline separates the dreamers from the doers.

You've seen it in every chapter: showing up to spar, journaling through grief, checking your gear before a firefight, setting boundaries with your children. It's never about motivation. It's about showing up anyway.

Most people want results. Few want routine. But the person who's disciplined long enough? They get both.

3. Orange Belt — Courage: Move Through Fear

Courage isn't the absence of fear—it's the refusal to let fear dictate your direction. At Orange Belt, you begin to engage. You move toward the fight instead of away from it.

Courage is asking for help. Ending the toxic relationship. Telling your kid, "I don't have all the answers." It's making the call, applying for the job, taking the first step, even when the outcome isn't guaranteed.

In the ring, fear shows up in your breathing. On the street, it lives in your hesitation. At home, it speaks in silence.

But if you move anyway? That's courage. It's action, not emotion.

Courage whispers, "Go." Fear screams, "Stay." And every time you choose to move, you rewrite the story of who you are.

4. Green Belt — Ego: Drop the Performance

The Green Belt is where growth becomes dangerous, because skill rises faster than wisdom. And that's when ego sneaks in.

You start to believe you've arrived. You want the credit. You crave the recognition. You confuse confidence with arrogance. That's ego. And ego will make you chase optics over outcomes.

Every time you tried to prove something to someone else in this book—whether in breakups, fights, or leadership—it ended in regret. Why? Because you forgot who you were doing it for.

Ego fights for validation. Growth fights for truth.

When you stop performing, you start progressing. When you stop defending your image, you start building your future.

Let go of being impressive. Start being real.

5. Blue Belt — Control: Return to Breath

Blue Belt is the first taste of real pressure. You've built competence, but now you must learn to be calm.

Control isn't rigidity. It's composure. It's taking the beat before you speak. It's breathing through stress. It's anchoring others by anchoring yourself.

In a firefight, a boardroom, or a family dinner, those who can regulate themselves influence everyone around them. Control is the pause between stimulus and response.

Without control, you react. With it, you respond.

You saw it on the roadside with the tire. In the ring, when panic hits. At the kitchen table with your child. The person who breathes first, wins second.

Inhale. Exhale. Own the space between.

6. Purple Belt — Responsibility: What You Do Affects Others

At Purple Belt, you begin to lead. But leadership isn't about position—it's about weight.

Responsibility means showing up when you don't feel like it. It means calming your child, not because you're calm—but because they need you to be. It means returning the call. Holding the standard. Being the steady one when others waver.

Responsibility is inconvenient. It asks more of you than you think you can give.

But every chapter showed us the same truth: someone else is always affected by how you act. On the mat. On the road. In your relationships. You're not just shaping your own life—you're shaping someone else's story.

Carry the weight. Without complaint. With honor.

7. Brown Belt — Mastery: Practice Without Applause

Brown Belt is not sexy. It's grind. It's polish. It's refining details no one sees.

Mastery is doing it again. Repeating the drill. Reviewing the loss. Training when it's lonely. Owning the nuance.

Mastery means studying the failure, not just celebrating the win. It means showing up when no one claps. It means having standards higher than what's required.

You don't rise by accident. You rise by repetition.

If discipline is doing it—mastery is doing it well. Consistently. Quietly. Without validation. You don't post about it. You just live it.

8. Black Belt — Legacy in Action: Be the Example

Black Belt is not the end. It's the beginning of being watched.

Legacy in action means someone is learning from how you live. By how you carry yourself in defeat. By how you speak to people who can't help you. By how you raise your kids, shake hands, and walk through life.

Legacy is lived, not written.

You don't always know who's watching. But someone is. A friend. A kid. A stranger. They're taking notes—not on your words, but your walk.

Be worth watching even when no one claps.

9. Red Belt — Legacy in Spirit: Become the Echo

The Red Belt is rare. It's for those who didn't just learn the system, but became it. Not many arrive here. That's why it matters.

Legacy in spirit is what lingers after you leave. It's not what you did—it's who you were. It's not what you said—it's how you made others feel.

In every chapter, the Red Belt lesson was this: you're building an echo. Make it worth hearing.

Will your presence be missed because of what you gave—or what you withheld?

The Red Belt isn't something you wear. It's something you are. And it only comes to those who lived by the rules long after the teaching ended.

Final Reflection: The Belt Rack

Picture the rack.

White. Yellow. Orange. Green. Blue. Purple. Brown. Black. Red.

Each belt frayed. Faded. Stained with effort. A story sewn into cotton.

You didn't earn these colors in the ring. You earned them in heartbreak, in parenthood, on the roadside, in the battle-field of your mind. You earned them in silence. In action. In consistency.

And now, the belts don't just tell a martial arts story.

They tell your story.

This isn't a book about fighting.

It's a book about living like you've trained. With humility, discipline, and courage. With composure, service, and truth. With mastery, legacy, and spirit.

The belts were never the goal.

Understanding was.

Now go—
Live like someone's learning.
Fight like someone's watching.
Love like it echoes forever.
And pass it on.

ABOUT THE AUTHOR

Professor Jason Figliano is more than a martial artist—he's a lifelong student of discipline, resilience, and human potential. A 6th-degree black belt in Karate and a 3rd-degree black belt in Brazilian Jiu-Jitsu under Master Royler Gracie, Jason has spent over two decades training, teaching, and mentoring students of all ages. Through his academies, business consulting, and public speaking, he's helped thousands of people sharpen not just their skills on the mat, but their confidence, mindset, and leadership off it.

Jason travels the world teaching martial arts seminars, delivering motivational keynotes, and consulting with business owners to help them scale with integrity and clarity. Whether he's speaking to a room full of CEOs or tying a white belt around a child's waist, Jason brings the same energy: lead with strength, live with purpose, and never settle for average.

His work extends far beyond martial arts. He's a successful entrepreneur, firearms safety instructor, and performance coach with a sharp mind for systems and an even sharper sense of accountability. Whether he's training law enforcement in control tactics or guiding a business through tough decisions, Jason's philosophy remains consistent—discipline and mindset are the ultimate equalizers.

He lives by two rules that shape his approach to life and leadership:

"People say you only live once. That's a lie. You only die once—but you live every single day. So make sure you actually live every single day."

"I never go with the flow—I flow with the go." What that means is simple: Going with the flow is like being dragged by a wave with no direction. But when you flow with the go, you've got the surfboard—you're in control, navigating the current on your own terms.

Jason is also a strong believer in traditional values and the natural balance between masculine and feminine energy. His views on leadership, family, and legacy are rooted in faith, clarity, and purpose—not postmodern trends.

ABOUT THE PUBLISHER

Dear Reader,

As you hold this remarkable book in your hands, we want to express our heartfelt gratitude for becoming a part of the Live Life Happy Community of readers. Your curiosity and thirst for knowledge fuel our passion for publishing meaningful non-fiction works.

At Live Life Happy Publishing, our mission is rooted in bringing forth literature that not only entertains but uplifts, supports, and nourishes the soul. We firmly believe that books have the power to transform lives, to ignite passions, and to spread joy far and wide.

Behind every word, every chapter, lies the dedication of our authors who pour their hearts and souls into their craft. Their ultimate aim? To touch your life in profound ways, to inspire, and to leave an indelible mark on your journey.

Your role in this journey is invaluable; by sharing your thoughts through reviews, spreading the word to others, or reaching out to the authors themselves, you become an integral part of sparking transformation in countless lives, igniting a ripple effect of joy and enlightenment.

And if, perchance, you or someone you know has dreams of writing, of sharing a message, or of unleashing a powerful story unto the world, know that Live Life Happy Publishing stands ready to guide you. Our doors are open, our ears attuned, and our hearts eager to hear your message.

So, dear reader, let us, continue to spread the power of literature, one page at a time. Reach out, share, and most importantly, never underestimate the power of your message to touch lives.

With warmest regards,

LiveLifeHappyPublishing.com

P.S. Remember, books change lives. Whose life will you touch with yours?

LiveLifeHappy
Publishing

www.ingramcontent.com/pod-product-compliance
Lightning Source LLC
Chambersburg PA
CBHW072127090426
42739CB00012B/3099